# Locus of Control
# Therapy Poems

## Rebecca Herz

© Rebecca Herz

Prolific Pulse Press LLC, Publisher
Published January 2026
Raleigh, North Carolina USA



This book is a fiction work. All names, characters, places, and incidents are products of the author's imagination. Any resemblance to actual people, living or dead, is unintentional and coincidental.

Permission requests are to be directed to:
Admin@prolificpulse.com

ISBN 978-1-962374-70-5 Paperback
ISBN 978-1-962374-71-2 ePub

Library of Congress Control Number: 2025927029

## Dedication

*Dedicated to the creators of the world. You are change-makers and healers, essential to our collective wellbeing. Never forget that.*

Thank you to everyone who made this book possible with your unwavering support. You know who you are, but I want to acknowledge you anyway:

To my wife, Jordana – Once again, you have been such a rock during this process. This book was three years in the making, and you are always respectful of my creative space while showing genuine curiosity and care for my art. Thank you always.

Of course, thank you to my friends and family, who tolerate and even embrace my onslaught of emails asking for opinions, insight, and suggestions on my poems. I know that I bombard you constantly with material you may or may not have the time to read, but you do it anyway. I just want to share my work with the people I love most, because at the end of the day, the work would be nothing without you.

Thanks to my teachers and mentors over the last twenty-so years since I became obsessed with my craft, for making it clear that artmaking is healing. I do my best to transmit these lessons to my young clients, and now to you, my readers.

Thank you to Lisa, whose appreciation for my work has been instrumental in building my confidence as a writer. We share a social work degree and get one another. I think that's what makes our professional relationship so special and energizing.

I also want to thank my therapy clients, whose middle school trials and tribulations inspire me each day to be of service to the younger generation. I often tell them, many of them artists in their own right, that artmaking should always draw from a source of self-love. I like to call the time and space given to creative acts a radical act of self-care. I have learned, and I share this as often as I can, that artmaking can help us self-actualize.

As the psychologist Maslow said, self-actualization is the final and highest tier on the hierarchy of needs. We are, in a way, always working toward this with our attempts to attain the primary tiers which represent basic needs. I have been surprised by how rarely our basic needs are truly met, and my purpose as a social worker and licensed therapist is to help my clients become in touch with and attain their honest needs.

I truly believe that therapy can't be taught any more than art can be taught. We all have the innate ability and desire to help ourselves and others achieve security and happiness. I find so much joy in the creative process I have stopped caring about impressing others with the end product.

May we all learn to fill our own cups so that we may become a source of support for others.

Last but most, thank you Ori Solomon, my littlest love, our baby boy. Know you are always home with Ima and Mommy. You are my greatest inspiration and deepest hope. May your life be filled with wonderful and radical acts of creative freedom.

*All personal proceeds from this book will be donated to the nonprofit Jewish Queer Youth (JQY) in support of LGBTQ children and teens.*

## Table of Contents

"Wherever you go, there you are."

—Jon Kabat-Zinn

## Attachment

My friend's 6-year-old son loves rare birds.
They're like dinosaurs, he says.
Dinosaurs don't exist, only birds do.
His eyes lock on mine.

I nod in agreement and when he smiles
I can see he's self-assured, unlike me.
Then he asks if I can read him a book
about the Hoatzin, which he says is his favorite bird.

He has a mohawk, the child beams, pointing to the page.
He asks me to read this information twice, and I do.
But when I ask if he'd like to visit the Hoatzin,
the child shakes his head.

I just like reading about birds, he counters.

It becomes clear, he does not wish to meet his hero
with binoculars and a camera.
Unlike me, he has no desire to capture nature.
It seems his philosophy can be boiled down to this:

Nature is not ours.
Birds are beyond our capacity, as nature's colonizers,
to love.

## Transference

A few weeks ago, the fertility clinic
did our expensive bidding,
merging our donor's Anglo-Saxon sperm
with my wife's Ashkenazi eggs.

Thank God, they made nine viable embryos,
and one will be implanted today.
We pray it'll stick,
unlike the last four.

Just this morning, I helped my wife press
the progesterone liquid through a syringe,
the long, thick needle penetrating the skin.

It's kind of surreal to know:
we now have a 75% likelihood of success,
a statistic we doubt, but we are playing cool.

In Jewish law, it's clear an embryo is not a being.
though if a Jewish boy is born dead,
He must be circumcised, then buried.

I guide my wife through visualization.
Imagine the baby in your arms, I say.
Hear its cry, touch its toes one by one

I hold her where the child is and wait.

**Active Listening**

Two nights ago, an army helicopter collided
with an American Airlines jet.
It's all over the news.

Loved ones demand answers
for the fireball that destroyed sixty-seven lives:
parents, children, pilots, and attendants.

None of us were ever guaranteed survival.

I scroll while listening for sirens
to light the freezing night.

## Positive Regard



My client, a sixth grader cut class again.
She said it was to ask an urgent question.
Turns out she forgot it, so I could not answer.
Instead, I gave her a pretzel, then wrote her a pass.

Later, she returned with vehemence, fire in her eyes,
except this time, she was skipping a test, so I asked why.
She said, *I don't know. I don't know. I don't know.*
I told her I understood, though I'm still not sure I did.

**Radical Acceptance**

6 | P a g e

Everyone transfers something.
When I was seven, my parents hired a therapist
who transferred his problems through me
like I was a battery.

In school they tell us to sure up and
subvert ourselves to the common good.
We learn we are conduits for pain.

My students knock on the door all day
with questions I know well
from years asking them.

In the rush between classes,
I see their downcast eyes -
I see their struggle as my own.

This is yet another week of contradictions
I cannot reconcile.
This work
has taught me the truth about ethics:

Wrong and right converse all night over coffee,
formulating arguments that make no sense,
only to disappear before dawn breaks.

**Imposter Syndrome**

7 | Page

Generation Alpha draws chalk figures on my board,
laughing with ambivalent smiles.

I am the therapist, meant to draw lines to a logical conclusion.
I was trained in a vast, uncharted Zoomiverse
to care.

A teacher pulled me aside yesterday
to ask me about her student.
He's safe, I said, not mentioning the ER.
I could not say the student showed sufficient evidence
for imminent threat.

This work can't be taught.

## Cultural Competence

8 | Page

They say my Papa wasn't a religious man.

His prayer shawl, torn, has since been mended.
The tassels, frayed, are still intact.

I wear his old-world dreams on my shoulders.

I've almost keeled over from too much prayer,
though I've forgotten how to pray.

The rabbi said his phylacteries aren't kosher.

They hide in a velvet bag up on the shelf.

I'll figure out how to fix them.

One time, I met a cousin in Jerusalem,
daughter of a big deal Rabbi, somehow family.

Like Papa always said, all of our people are connected.

**Positive Psychology**

I try to see a little of everything,
to make all matters matter to me.

I wonder at the robin, and marvel
at the sea.
I buy each and every pedagogy,

I become one with bird and bee.
Though I'm ignorant of beak and stinger,
on each verse I'll parse and linger.

Yet my inner world remains sparse.

I cannot tell my own thoughts from yours,
my own breath from the breeze.

I yearn to put my heart at ease.

Positive Psychology

## Self-Compassion

God, take a walk with me.

Pause with me to gaze at every bird.
We'll wonder if the cardinal is auspicious,
or simply red.

Dispel all questions.
Allow doubt to float off on the breeze.

Not that you pause, gaze, doubt,
wonder or even walk.

You have no questions for nature.

Rose means rose.
Dirt means dirt.

Root my fingers through the earth.

You do not judge, smile, laugh,
or scoff. You simply witness your reflection
in all things.

**Locus of Control**

There is very little to do about most things,
no way to silence nature when it sings.

Few changes remain possible in the world we've co-created.
At times, it seems God is set on making us lie in the bed we made.

Yet we can't blame God for this constant clutter of casualties,
We have always been hoarders of tragedies.

**Shadow Self**

If fate is a puppet's shadow on a blank wall,
destiny must be the shape each shadow takes.

It is a helpless feeling to watch the dance that can't be stopped,
blind to the hands on the strings, pulling and resting, pulling and
resting.

Shadow Self

**Existentialism**

I am an image of myself,
copied and pasted,
cruelly interchangeable.

I am no star, but common
Starling, peanut, and not pearl.

It doesn't matter anymore.

I am in love.

**Reclamation**

We do not have a name for our love,
no term of endearment to hide it in.
Marriage was not made for us.

There's no groom to speak of,
only male factor infertility,
and the imagined face of a child
half your own, not really mine -
at least not by blood.

Tomorrow in the sterile room,
the ultrasound tech will label our child
with medical terms we can't decode.

It's true, no primordial woman in her loincloth
spread her legs under hospital fluorescents,
though she did scream the heaviest
scream, the one you will scream
before breaking.

Reclamation

**Unmasking**

Spent so much time editing,
I forgot to create.

Revised too far, too soon,
and lost the essence
of the craft, which is to feel
all the guts and be real.

I could not allow myself
the space for true art.
I was worried to death I'd confuse you
with my oddities and blasphemies.

Well, here I am,
untethered from approval.

Now read me, touch my unkempt words -
embrace, or don't.

I'll be here anyway, oblivious with joy.

**Doorknob Confession**

I see no evil, though it sees me
through all illusion.

I'm here wading through apocalyptic streams
like the rest, no reprieve from news blasts and rocket fire.

There's no time, or space, between the objective and desire.

We sit in a circle at the ethics meeting,
chanting our sins into the vacancy.

Our prayers are splitting God's hairs.

## Non-Judgmental Stance



It took billions of years to set the scene,
then, the stage manager left.

Now we're caught trying to catch our rhythm,
the beat established long ago.

I don't want to spend all my time searching
for the state of mind I'm meant to have.

I'm done practicing choreography, then preaching originality.

Authenticity seems futile when we're taught
to listen without judgement.

I only open my mouth when necessary.

It's been years since I've offered
my true opinion.

**Shame**

The instructions for living
caught fire in a dumpster.

This loss was inevitable.

We saw the sirens and took the hint,
staying away from danger.

We could not restrain it
as it crept toward us.

I remember wishing -
for what, I'm not clear.

Whoever set the book aflame
has forgotten shame.

Shame

**Faith**

I've always wanted to find you,
so, I spent years decoding your signs.

At times, you were my only friend.

I've tried to track you down,
studied all things divinity.

Life is harder than ever,
so many revelations squashed.

My belief in you is, most often, in the past.

**Reframe**

Scientists at The Rubin Observatory
count on life beyond our galaxy.
In a way, so do we.

Twenty billion distinct universes exist.
Likely more, and we are at war.

We are at war.
Pan over the flames
with a wide lens, don't look too close.

Stars explode every millisecond,.
if seen, it would destroy our vision.

All this in the name of religion.

Beyond our galaxy I imagine calm, cool, collected lives,
perhaps animated rocks, unfeeling, never hurt,
not requiring healing.

They are simply a piece in the mosaic of nebulae.

Yet no mosaic of nebulae can capture us:
no expertise, no mathematics, not
any field of view, old or new.

Is our humanity relevant here?
We are all huddled in a knot.

Zoom in close enough, you'll find,
at the corner of millennia,

time and space collapse in moments.
We are nothing but a speck on screen.
All we can see is but a near invisible
aspect of Truth. Our love is a microcosm
of what Love is. I wonder if we
will ever find out who we are to Love.

**Surrender**

We are meant to trust in God.
In faith, it's blasphemous to panic.

There are so many forms of blasphemy,
numerous ways to get excommunicated.

I am willing to jump the fence barring
free will from destiny, and fall.

I don't mind the dirt under my fingernails,
or the crops half-drowned by this year's cicadas
whose casings remind me of walnut shells.

In the beginning, before death and destruction,
we floated on a raft in the middle of the sea.

There, we felt safer
than even now, which is saying a lot.

No one floats on their back for hours
without riding a few risky waves.

Not one of us gets by without close calls.
A canoe will capsize at least once for the avid rower.

The more passionate we are, the more of ourselves we are ready to
risk.
We will all get the feeling that there is nothing left to lose.

Yet there is, more often than not, little choice.
We must pretend to have a say when it's clear we don't.

I have my teenage clients list the pros and cons
until there's nothing left to list, and reflect

on the cost-benefit of every move. I'm sure,
though I do not let on, there is no decision but acceptance.

No one will see the changes they seek all at once.
It's lucky if we even have the means to hope for change at all.

Followers of the Middle Way demonstrate how equilibrium
can save a soul, yet it seems there is no balance in sight.

We are couched these days between two extremes,
dancing in and out of each one without thought.

Here's my creed: Always hang in the doorway,
but never step fully into the room.
In there live the shadows we abandoned as children.

I used to hold onto my shadow for dear life, then left
her back home with my helplessness.

I became a hollow cell where the weeds grow taller
than redwoods, wilder than a field untouched for decades.

Marley said not to worry, but I cannot believe him,
even when repeated on a loop for years, I don't know

If these words can stand the test of time,
especially these times, I'll be surprised.

Awe is a strange thing. I can't connect
with fear, but awe gives me enough reason to love.

## Forgiveness

It's possible to cover an entire floor with white paint,
smudge it around with little fingers and laugh.

Quite likely, we will whitewash all that is
and forget what we did in time for dinner.

Money is culprit and key to success,
yet you allow me to doubt this.

You challenge me to care for more than material,
dissolve my jealousy, with grace.

You call me out, teach me my privilege is a broken branch.
I hold it while lying on the ground, though it is rotting
with this year's storms and infestations. I pray
for another chance to prove I am willing to change.

Thank God, you don't buy it, instead,
you carry my backpack, hold my water bottle.

As I lift myself off the forest floor once again,
you smile at me and start to laugh, so I smile and laugh.

All our trouble melts in a pool of wax,
the approval I seek, vaporized.

**Refocus**

You say I am distractible.
No kidding,
though I say I focus on what matters.

Robins collect refuse to house their babies.
Groundhogs seek refuge in the boroughs they dig.
Squirrels attack the bird feeders, spilling seeds.

I ask if your love is retractable,
and even if the answer is no,
I won't believe you.

Yet life goes on:
The turtle hides in its calloused shell.
A small guitar plays in the background,
some Bach or Steely Dan,
until the world is still once more.

**Compassion Fatigue**

To some, love is a secret
to which no one has access,
except for them.

To others, love is a hollow rock,
beaten for water until their hands bleed,
the striking stick split in two.

I am not one to guess what love is
or isn't, I simply observe how it flows
in and out, an ever more tumultuous tide.

When the waves break, the foam rises.
I see love in the time it takes for them to crash,
turning to wet sand. I am no longer adrift
on the tiny raft of gathered sticks I made
when I was a child.

In making my peace with the demolition
of childhood hopes, I conjure an image
of a love I cannot articulate here.

If we were all love's servants, we'd be fine,
though our roles are yet to be defined.
I hold onto you like my life depends on it.

You have helped me to understand the nature
of love, that I must ride the waves to last,
until I learn to swim far past the ebb and flow.

## Trauma-Informed

I've watched the twitch of an ear,
curious, unsettled, and confused
by what it's asked to hear.

Many times, I've seen and felt
how the body urges silence out of exile.
I'm finding it harder to smile.
I fear they'll misunderstand.
I did not intend to portray
the meanings painted over my face.

My expression betrays my better judgement.
I am together only until I fall apart,
my hidden truth, revealed in art.
I can't explain my truth in conversation,
only verse
makes it possible for anyone to know me.

Fold over the page and find the spot
where all my truths lie waiting.

Until my true self spills over the binding
like an unspooled thread.

**Co-Regulation**

We could not understand each other. Though we tried to explain
our reasoning, it was always unreasonable to the other.

You were on the other side of a river that wouldn't stop rushing.
I was on a rock waving to you, but you couldn't see or hear.

On the other side, there is always bright green grass and dandelions,
whether or not the person there is right.

I've thought before, for a moment, maybe no one is right.
You are possibly an echo of my former self.
She, of course, disagrees with everything I say.
In that case I would be your shadow.

I follow you around, clingy, unaware
of my surroundings, the exits
non-existent over the blank expanse.

I wanted to speak my truth, but forgot
how.

You were always asking me to feel the way you felt,
to act the way you wanted me to act.

I was never enough for you, and you
were never enough for me.

So, we sat down for dinner and decided to try.
Many times, we sat, spoke, and processed
the wounds from way before we met, reaching from down,
down below our feet.
Like roots that wrap and choke a young sequoia,
our marriage was a victim of growth and change.

We learned to recognize this, and forgive
the healing, however long it would take.

Our pain was just the healing taking its time,
rushing through the channels of our consciousness.

We stand on the same side, together, watching
with wonder as the waters leap forward,
covering and covering the hurt like a billowing sheet.
The burns cooling with persistence, developing scabs.
The nature of love is to heal itself,
it is regenerative.
Sever a limb and it'll grow back. Even if you burn the tree,
all the bark in a smooth pile of ash, there will be regrowth.
This is the way of renewal, the human spirit all encompassing.

Lichen forms on the rock, and once again,
The flames unspool into healing waters.

We bend to touch the moss, to lie
in the bed we have made for ourselves

We sleep on the chest of the earth,
listen to its gentle heartbeat, together.

Our hands, intertwined,
set us free from the dangers of night.

Listen to the rocking of the waves, the tide
turning in and out, a vortex of truths
Neither of us knew before we met.

We sink our toes into the clay of the moving
storm, the muddied earth, a puddle at our feet.

We sit on a rock and wait for the arrival of daylight.

## The Unsaid

I'd rather play the bongo in my living room,
wrapped in a blanket and picking at chips.

Would rather take the local train home,
to revel in the beauty of the long way.

Don't tell me I'd rather be saving lives,
or picking up trash from the street.

Tell me it won't be long before I find myself
squishing sneakers in mud through the woods.

Won't be forever before I take my own path,
carve out a byway all my own and follow

the drumbeats of my own heart,
the drummer smiling within.

Show me I am not a pawn in someone else's game,
someone who never explained the rules or told me my role.

We are a revolving door of dreams.
To be human is to move through the endless loop

of wishes and commands. We are air
through the brush, the end of the path

covered in fresh mowed grass, once a cemetery,
leveled for convenience and forgotten.

**Effacement**

Here, there used to be a certain species of bird
that would not fly unless you flew ahead,
that shed its feathers in flight, so all at once
it was naked, scorched by sunlight.

I do not know how to lead, I wasn't taught
to love myself as my neighbor, but the opposite.

Forgiveness was always the way to go.
Caring little for my own needs, I fled
from myself, with a one-way ticket
to an imaginary golden palace in the ether.

Either I'm a slave to my circumstances,
or a queen on the throne of fate.

It's only an illusion, bravery.
There's no courage but the will to survive
another day, so we can start again,
unencumbered by today's nonsense.

We prioritize our own, those we love,
while the stranger does not exist,
does not matter at all.

My personal scripture tells me
to cover my mouth when I speak,
to stifle all signs of emotion,
ignore the truth I seek.

As I've gotten older, I've forgotten how to stop
caring. I've learned to fly ahead of the flurry of activity
year after year,
so I don't have to ask why I'm here.

**Burnout**

One cup of coffee is not enough and too much.
My shaking hands focus only on themselves.
As I navigate the burning fortress of my mind,
ashes to ashes, my thoughts are on fire.

I attempt to heal the broken, yet I am too
broken to heal, at least it seems so.
I am told that anything is possible:
I only have to conform to the norm.

I am taking two steps backward every time I move,
falling so suddenly in and out of love.
All I want is freedom from my own trappings,
to embrace what is with utmost grace.

At times, I yearn to leave this place,
if only to dance among my own
unfettered, to lie in a field of weeds,
and love them all like precious flowers.

**Uncertainty**

Scan the earth for gold,
then, when you hit it,
feel everything.
Let the pleasure of finding a pulse still your heart.
Watch your gift unfold,
a gift that does not belong to you,
but to the earth or something higher.
It does not belong to the sky or the clouds,
not the sun or the celestial sphere,
but higher still.

Or maybe all of presence exists
on a plane of shock and serendipity.

Witness the blossoming of life,
a masterpiece:
petal and nectar,
fat and bone.

As they guide the probe over the skin,
you are reveling in prehistory,
meanings that have not yet existed.
The future is unveiling before your eyes
in pixelated frames, marked
in yellow on a screen.

You remain just distant enough
not to feel its heartbeat on your chest.

**Vigilance**

Will this child have the strength to speak,
to walk, to dance?
All of this is yet to be known.

No guarantees: a picture is a picture,
a human being the measure of its meaning,
not its parts.

In dreams you see a child, covered in moonlight,
or fluorescents, transferred as a bundle of cells
with the utmost fear,
which is the first expression of love.
A mother can only ask, can I call you mine?
Are you human? Or an alien
from a long-forgotten planet
on the other side of a wormhole?

You look at the sonogram and see the northern lights,
a disco, the greatest celebration
of human potential and nature.
You hope for the alien's wellbeing
how a heart wills itself to beat.

You pray for its safe arrival
as a lung longs for breath.

A mother can only ask,
How can I bring you here into my arms
right now, without destroying you?
There is no way.

You must wait patiently
as a child on the stoop,
listening with the utmost intensity
for the ice cream truck.
Pray there won't be sirens.
It will take nine minutes.
It will take nine months.

For now, the screen is vibrant. Watch the shifting shapes,
the tangled web of forms expressed in black and white,
photographs which will later be printed and put into a folder,
for safekeeping.
This is terrifying,
there is no way around it.
Terror is the first step,
then forgiveness of the terror
and the one who caused it.
What else is a mother supposed to do
but let the terror pass,
and hope to God she's not swept up with it?

To separate a mother from her love
is to rip a picture into shreds.
To keep a mother from her child
is to break off a piece of her heart.

Before a child is born, make sure to mourn.

**Twin Flames**

Tonight, my guitar is a child in my arms.
At once, I recognize the dissonance
between holding sacred and holding close.

The sacred is a song in my heart.
Those sanctified among us, mere relics,
were never mine to keep.

In the silences between songs,
I feel the beyond wrap around me,
embracing me in pure white light.

The light is fire, comforting
my inner traveler, weary with wanderlust.
I hold my calloused hands over the flame and wait.

I can see the end:
a firewall the full length of the universe.
The burning fortress speaks softly. It says,

Your journey ends here.
As the flame inches closer to my open hands,
it asks me to hold it as I would a child.

The flame is music raging through the earth.
At the bottom of the ocean, it still burns,
holding me in its melody all my life.

Now that the guitar is a child in my hands,
I rock his tears away and pray he sleeps.
His tears mark the beginning of a resolution,

To measure the music with my whole body,
to beat the flames of sound with my bare hands.
I contemplate the menial with nowhere to go.

Here is the sacred vibration, the cleansing chord,
held for centuries, strummed into the stars.
I'll meet you in paradise with music in my arms.

I promise to play you exactly how you ask,
you don't have to move a muscle.
I will hold you as long as I live.

You are the lyric, light and dark.
Tonight, you battle against
the inner and outer flames

with nothing more than a whisper.
We echo all over without a care,
shadows of our former selves.

Maybe it is some sort of miracle
to experience the sacred like this.
I suppose not everyone gets the chance

to love beyond capacity, expand
past reason into the ether,
to become the atmosphere.

Together, first you, then me,
we are waiting for the signal
to hold our ears to the earth.
We will listen for its heartbeat,
the thrums and patterns
reflected in our bodies.

If the divine fashioned us,
there must be no separation
between bodies, hearts, and souls.

Strange that music has always been our glue,
sacred vibrations that resonate throughout
the world and connect us all to humanity.

You are merely one in the crowd.
In my dreams, I elbow through a mob
to reach, to touch, to embrace you.

I can't do without this electricity,
holding us together.

## Non-Duality

There will come a day light and dark will blend,
and nobody will know the difference
between day and night, sea and sky.

You'll draw near again, once and for all,
then, once you return, no one will have to miss you.
No confusion anymore, just a found sense
of wisdom that's never felt possible.

I want to meet you on the longest path,
the only way to meet you.

Forgotten or simply denied recognition,
you have rested in exile billions of years.
Even the stars have lost faith.

To those who feel you everywhere,
I ask, *Where did you get the heartfelt
sense you are pervaded by peace?
When did you realize
peace was not only in your mind?*

You share yourself with the divine and have nothing left.

We are all one and other, inseparable.

In fact, there is no other.
And if there is no true other.

We are One.

**Social Skills**

If I approach with trepidation, know
it's out of reverence, not fear.

The way I reach out is in.
I read the face the way others read a foreign language.

If I pronounce your meaning without words,
incoherent and impossible to tell

my want from your need, I will try
again, though I cannot guarantee results.

My mind is an oven full of unleavened bread,
burning furnace of confusion.

The meanings are mangled, melted flat
in what can only be called an echo chamber

of self. My mind is the only theory, my theory
the only mind that matters to me.

Oh, how I strain to know you,
want to see you, yearn to feel how you feel.

So, if I seem aloof, don't assume I'm a lost cause -
I want to connect however I can.

If nothing else, know this:
around your true expression is a fence

I would jump if only I could.
Someday, I hope to tear it down for good.

I would jump if only I could.

**Complacency**

The fridge broke last night.
We woke up to disaster.

All the valuables must go.
Nothing can be salvaged.

We had planned it out so well:
cubed meat, chopped potatoes.

Disaster is, of course, relative.
Wasted food is not a catastrophe.

We cannot mourn what was never ours.
If lost, it was not meant to be.

We will call the fixer,
evaluate the broken mechanism.

There will be more loss, for sure,
some cost to mend what's necessary.

There's no choice.
We must return to the status quo.

Supermarket splurges, inflated bills,
fruit that rots as soon as it is bought.

We never learn, not really,
though it seems we've wizened up, we haven't.
We are part of the machine that fuels progress,
allowing crimes to which we'd never consciously consent.

## Borderline



I always misinterpret the signs.
The lines on your face are simply lines.
When you squint your eyes from the sun,
furrow your brow in confusion,
I feel alone deep in my soul.
The initial hurt determines all.

The first loss is the primary fear.
I've been running away from the proverbial bear.
The primary hurt determines every move.
I fail in friendships and in love.
You're the only star in my galaxy,
until the victim child takes over my body.

There's always the forest, already the bear,
chasing my tail and raising every hair.
My heart palpitates with pain.
I race for shelter, always on the run.
You are the safety, you are the hurt
to the inner prey I must revert.

I lost you the moment I chose to trust,
in reverence to pain our love will combust.
A rose is a rose: it's possible to break
the pattern of misinterpretation. I ache
to reveal my heart, to separate
the trauma from my art.

Between two selves a border stands,
separating disparate lands.
No soul has yet crossed over,
no parent, friend, or lover.
It's a portal I am yearning to step though:
the only way I'll make it is with you.

## Lucid Dreams

47 | Page

I try to open my eyes, but they want to remain closed.
Light is streaming through the curtains, while my dreams
stay in sight like clouds I cannot reach.

Some people can control their dreams.
More lucid than in daylight they form.
They never want to leave their dreams.

Behind the veil of night is a compromise:
to wake would be to lose the magic.
I do not want to lose my will to dream.

My love fills my dreams with wanting
that falls apart the moment day breaks.
I forget my desire with the first light.

In the middle of the day, I close my eyes again.
Dreams play behind my eyelids, and I sense their weight.
Someday these dreams will come to live outside of me.

**Transformation**

I wanted to become a butterfly
without the years of yearning.

I needed wings a long time ago,
the body of an angel.

I trap myself in my cocoon,
to someday fly.

To emerge wings first out of the wreckage,
once and for all.

## Inner Child

Where did she go – the child I was,
who sang over the din of the school bus,
Who chased time with a stopwatch?

She has gone missing – I was frantic
running after her through the schoolyard,
when she disappeared into the shadows.

I am sure she hopped the fence
and is hiding in the honeysuckle bush,
sipping nectar from the tiny buds.

Missing her, I forget my name:
the story I tell about my future
is rooted in her mind.

**Mindfulness-Based**

I am trying to be mindful
to notice the robin on the brush,
and follow her with eyes wide open
as she flits from branch to branch.

I am trying to see everything,
to root in the earth,
blossom with the roses.

I fall short of the mindfulness required
to sense the cosmos in my bones.

Instead, I find myself alone
beside a concrete wall, typing
in a gray, fluorescent room.

Mindfulness-Based

## Rock Bottom

With nothing left to do, I find myself adrift,
holding onto a fallen branch.
There is only so long I can float.
I hear the water rushing over the edge.

Treading water with my feet,
I hear the water rushing over the edge and cry out.
You may or may not hear me, but do not respond.
There is only so long I can float here without sinking.

Holding onto a fallen branch, the waterfall engulfs
the air with vapor. I breathe it all in.
There is no world other than the waterfall.
Time is water rushing over the edge.

**Radical Amazement**

The elevator is broken so I take the stairs.

Drills resound in the hollow space
between floors.

I reach the third,
turn the key and open the red door,
feed the cats their tuna and chicken.

Then I brew my decaf coffee, find the couch,
delete all the voicemails from insurance bots,
turn on the robot vacuum, load the dishwasher,
make my peanut butter sandwich, and lint roll my pants.

The doorbell rings: I open the door.
She's changing out of her scrubs. She sat in a patient's pee.

She asks me about my day. I say it was good, though it was just ok.

We sit and eat in our pajamas. She likes the food and thanks me,
the same thing every Thursday, but she likes it so I make it.

Finally, we take off our rings and jump in the shower,
dry off, get back into our pajamas, call some people, and lie down.

She kisses me, and we embrace.

We fall asleep in each other's arms,
forgetting, thank God, what we lack.

**Prayer**

She takes her prayer as she takes her coffee.
To her, it is ordinary.

Her book, torn in spots,
holds the traditions
worn with years.

The pages are soft,
the binding messed up.

She doesn't notice,
prays as if nobody's watching.
Is anybody watching?

To her, it's as if prayer
is a passage to a faraway land of pleasure and pain,
with all her longing manifest through its expression.

**Projection**

I watched the workman stare at the sun.
His gaping mouth suggested fear.
I was taking my recycling,
ignoring the whole spectacle.

Some people drove for hours to watch
the total eclipse, the last one in our lifetime.
And here I was with my chore,
against the darkening sky.

There was something beautiful
about the workman
watching the eclipse on duty.
I projected fear.
Convinced he felt the same as me.

I took out my eclipse glasses
and stared at the sliver of the sun under darkness.

It was underwhelming at first.
I felt a sense of disappointment.
Was I looking at the same sun as the workman?

It was like watching a dream covered in a curtain,
a sliver of it left.
Maybe the workman saw the same dream
playing shadows across his face.

Or was it my dream
that I projected onto the cosmos?

**Questioning**

I want to ask the moon
if it yearns to be the sun,
to open a book and question
every last word on the page.

I live to replace the mundane
with the holy and the holy
with the mundane. I yearn to see
the forest from the shadows of trees.

Questions, not answers
fill the space between my prayers.
The electricity between my fingers
is its own magic.

I hope only to lie in the wild
flowers and sing to a God
I do not understand,
all day and all night forever.
I long to dance with the bees
and feel the buzzing in my bones.
To feel alive, alive, and free
in my mortal, fragile body.

Questions fill the caverns
of my daydreams with yearning,
echoing through the emptiness,
until there is finally fullness.

**Self-Help**

Recently, I've spent all my mornings listening
to the Happiness Podcast,
turning my wheels to talk of gratitude,
which only exists in children's journals.
I listen so often, so intently
I've come to transcend myself.

A Harvard expert presents the data.
The voiceover says we're distrustful and afraid,
and that there is a statistically significant
decline in happiness,
as if happiness were a statistic
and not a state of the soul.

My headphones have become crutches.
Placing them over my ears midday,
my lunch break turns into an opportunity.
The camaraderie of the podcast
is most filling.
I avoid the lunchroom,
preferring the expertise of those
who recommend socializing to the act itself.

The podcast teaches me:
make neighbors into friends,
become a better person, and
harness the power of connection.
I am still listening when I return
to a home dark and still,
from when I begin to cook
to when I scrub the last of the dishes.

The Happiness Podcast sings me to sleep,
a lullaby so soothing I forget to think.
I fall asleep to impossible advice,
then wake again, and again,
wholly myself.

**Watching the Clock**

I'd go so far as to say I am incapable
of keeping time – I have never understood how.
Time is not an object I can turn,
in my hand, and it is not a thing to own.

Analog clocks always kept me
longing for the next minute,
the lines between moments faint.
How does one distinguish between them?

When time is filled, I am content.
Yet, when empty, time feels purposeless.
The waiting game has never suited me.
One day blends seamlessly into the next,
till year-to-year is all one yearning.

We are expected to make meaning,
all our milliseconds accounted for.
I am no expert at this task,
which at times feels impossible.

Some days it is like filling a balloon
then letting it go in midair.
I often miss the mark by a hair.
My watch is a little off, and I fail.
My alarm forgets to ring, I am late.
Mistakes befall me and humble my spirit.

I wish I knew how
to read time
like God.
To see it for what it is...
and not what it seems to be.

**Disconnect**

You're going up while I'm going down.
I watch you go and call out,
but you cannot hear me.
There is no way to cross over.
You cannot see me,
as if there is a wall between us.

You look straight ahead.
Perhaps another realm waits
at the top and you're heading
toward the future with eyes open,
as I fall backward,
my eyes closed,
trusting no one.

**Disconnect**

**Attention to Detail**

I do my best not to waste a thing.
All objects have a byproduct of value.
It's a matter of attention to detail
of how a thing is made. Certain parts may be discarded
while others are used, even loved.

An Eagle Scout will eat an apple core
just to avoid leaving it on the trail.
A rope can be tied to a heart
and gifted instead of being burned.
Any person can either be saved or not.

I do not know of anything with nothing
to give, though there are works of art
that make no sense to the naked eye,
not to mention questions that are too opaque
to be answered in all honesty.

Time seems to be wasting away.
Every day, I open my eyes, and it slips
through my fingers. The moment
I hold them up to my face
and let the first light stream in, time is gone.

The magazine can be cut into pieces
before being thrown into a pile
and taken out with the trash.
The images can be glued on a vision board,
made to reflect our deepest desires.

Sacred meanings are salvaged -
meanings we did not see before.
Whenever an object is savored,
it can never be forsaken.
It is then like a still life forever captured.

**Grief**



Sundays, we would walk miles,
stop in diners for chocolate croissants,
feed pigeons from the benches
in Riverside park.

On Tuesdays, I'd always call,
your voice sultry, your smile
evident as we spoke Spanish. Later on,
you'd send me pictures of the pigeons.

I keep them alive in my phone,
now that you're gone.

**Collective Consciousness**

Another year's initial brightness dims.
We watch it go with boredom though we care
enough to prepare out of fear. Winter comes.
One day darkens another.

This year's deceit somehow becomes our creed,
an opaque film over our Collective Need.
Life, a smoke screen of worry, clouds our senses.
One day burdens another.

With the years, I lose hope against the flames
racing through the chambers of my mind.
I save what I can while I sound the alarm.
One day engulfs another.

With artificial wants and intelligent plans,
I form a firewall against the confession
that my inner landscape has turned to smoke.
One day revokes another

Who knows where the old year went?
It's whispering from elsewhere, urging me
to observe with concern, to know, to care.
One day reminds another.

We are learning to love one another. See
how we want to fight for our living
against the famine, floods, and flames?
One day recalls another.

We admire the earth and its creatures,
believe in beauty and in truth.
I plead with the earth to let me feel.
One day numbs another.

Warmth unburdens our apprehension.
We learn how to redeem our desolation,
though mystery decides the course of nature.
One day absolves another.

Cold comes. I navigate the dark
of downed trees and demolished homes.
Disaster looms. I watch and then deny.
One day grieves another.

Though we're hurt by the failure to admit
our faults, we bypass one another, and ourselves.
Fighting our common fate, we have to love.
One day forgives another.

One more minute, hour, day, and year
turn opaque in the eclipsed world.
I first observe powerless, then remember,
one day cleanses another.

Spring, the light returns. At once,
I feel the sun on my skin, the air between us
electrified, as your voice lingers in the space
you leave. One day reveals another.

The earth smells of lilacs, the dirt rich, cool to touch.
Even the ash comes to revive the dead.
For a moment, the smokescreen of fear dissolves.
One day frees another.

**Publishing Credits:**



I am a listed writer for the following publications on Medium: *Put It To Rest, My Fair Lighthouse, Genius in a Bottle, Writer's Bloke, of Poetry and People, Be Open, Resistance Poetry, The Happy Human, Prism & Pen, Way/Words Literary Journal*: a non-exhaustive list. I have so much gratitude to these publishers for putting out some of the first versions of the poems from this collection and from my first book, *Homecoming and other poems*. You can find my independently published works at rebeccaherzpoetry.medium.com and you can find Homecoming at prolificpulse.com/rebeccaherz.

**A blurb on *Homecoming and other poems*:**



The poems in this debut collection explore the depth of feeling of a poet in transition between continents, identities, and belief systems. Through real and imagined travels over the course of 5-years the work of these poems is to represent the coming of age, coming out, and coming home of a young poet. Finally, Homecoming is a question: who am I to my faith, and what is my faith to me? It is an answer: whoever you are your faith is your home. Whatever your path, whoever you are, Homecoming may just contain a part of yourself you've been hoping to meet.

## About the Author

Rebecca Herz is a poet, wife, new mom, cat lover, and school-based therapist. Her 2023 book, *Homecoming and other poems*, along with her social media content, can be found on linktr.ee/rebeccaherz. Her latest poetry collection, *Locus of Control* (2026), can be found on ProlificPulse.com/RebeccaHerz with links for purchase.

Thank you for reading Locus of Control.
Reviews are appreciated.

GoodReads

Amazon